HAL•LEONARD™
CORPORATION

7777 W. BLUEMOUND RD., P.O. BOX 13819 MILWAUKEE, WI 53213

ISBN 0-7935-8486-8

Photo's Pages 2, 3, 36, 37 Liz Johnson-Artur

Beetlebum

Beetlebum
What you done
She's a gun
Now what you've done
Beetlebum
Get nothing done
You beetlebum
Just get numb
Now what you've done
Beetlebum

And when she lets me slip away
She turns me on all my violence is gone
Nothing is wrong
I just slip away and I am gone
Nothing is wrong
She turns me on
I just slip away and now I am gone

Beetlebum
Because you're young
She's a gun
Now what you've done
Beetlebum
She'll suck your thumb
She'll make you cum'
Coz' she's your gun
Now what you've done
Beetlebum

He's on, he's on, he's on it

Song 2

I got my head checked
By a jumbo jet
It wasn't easy but nothing is
no

When I feel heavy metal
And I'm pins and I'm needles
Well, I lie and I'm easy
All the time but I am never sure
why I need you
Pleased to meet you

I got my head down
When I was young
It's not my problem
It's not my problem

When I feel heavy metal
And I'm pins and I'm needles
Well, I lie and I'm easy
All the time but I am never sure
why I need you
Pleased to meet you

Yeah Yeah
Yeah Yeah
Yeah Yeah
Oh Yeah

Country Sad Ballad Man

Yeah I found no where
It got to know me
Let me sleep all day
Spent the money
I haven't felt my legs
Since the summer
And I don't call my friends
Forgot their numbers

VIP 223
Have my chances
They have me
Now stay up nights
Watch TV
I'm country sad
I'm a ballad man

I'm on the come back road
Yeah I'm a bizzard
And in my motor home
Sweat on my pillow all night

I'm a ballad man . . .

M.O.R.

It's automatic
I need to unload
Under the pressure
Gone middle of the road
Fall into fashion
Fall out again
We stick together
Cause it never ends

Here comes a low
I'm a boy and you're a girl
Here comes a high
The only ones in the world
Here comes everything
You and me can work it out
Here it comes
You Me, we'll work it out!

Here comes tomorrow
1 2 3 episodes
The middle of the road
Cause that's entertainment
It's the sound of the wheel
It rolls on forever
You know how it feels

Here comes a low
I'm a boy and you're a girl
Here comes a high
The only one that's in the world
Here comes everything
We're like monkeys out in space
Here it comes
You Me, we'll work it out!

It's automatic
I need to unload
Under the pressure
Gone middle of the road
Fall into fashion
Fall out again
We stick together
Cause it never ends

Here comes a low
I'm a boy and you're a girl
Here comes a high
You're the one that's in the world
Here comes everything
You and me can work it out
Here it comes
You Me, we'll work it out!

On Your Own

Holy man tiptoed his way across the ganges
The sound of magic music in his ears
Videoed by a bus load of tourists
Shiny shellsuits on and drinking lemonade
Now I got a funny feeling which I bought mailorder
From a man in a teepee in California
Said he once was that great game show performer
Then he blew all his money away
Blew it all away

So take me home
don't leave me alone
I'm not that good
But I am not that bad
No psycho killer
Hooligan guerrilla
I dream to riot
Oh you should try it
I'll eat parole get gold card soul
My joy of life is on a roll
And we'll all be the same in the end

Then you're on your own (2)

Well we all go happy day glow in the disco
The sound of magic music in our brains
Someone stumbles to the bathroom with the horrors
Says' Lord give me time for I've jumped into space
I'm in outer space

So take me home
don't leave me alone
I'm not that good
But I am not that bad
No psycho killer
Hooligan guerrilla
I dream to riot
Oh you should try it
I'll eat parole get gold card soul
My joy of life is on a roll
And we'll all be the same in the end

Then you're on your own (2)

You're So Great

Sad drunk and poorly
Sleeping really late
Sad drunk and poorly
Not feeling so great
Wondering lost in a town full of frowns
Sad drunk and poorly
Dogs digging up the ground

And I feel the light in the night and in the day
And I feel the light when the sky's just mud and grey
And I feel the night when you tell me it's okay
Coz' you're so great and I love you

Tea, Tea and Coffee
Helps to start the day
Tea, Tea and Coffee
Shaking all the way
Cities alive, a surprise so am I
Tea, Tea and Coffee, get no sleep today

And I feel the light in the night and in the day
And I feel the light when the sky's just mud and grey
And I feel the night when you tell me it's okay
Coz' you're so great and I love you.

Death of a Party

The death of the party
Came as no surprise
Why did we bother
should have stayed away

Another night
And I thought well well
Go to another party
And hang myself
Gently on the shelf

The death of the teenager
standing on his own
why did he bother
should have slept alone

Another night
And I thought well well
Go to another party
And hang myself
Gently on the shelf

(Repeat)

Chinese Bombs

He makes an inner arm block
Then kicks from behind
The lights they go off
But he can fight blind
Coz' he got the touch
But he won't live long
Coz' he comes from Hong Kong
where people are strong

Chinese Bombs, millions jump, chairman's junk, USA
Won't Somebody, Won't Somebody
Sink the place

Got a cab to go to Soho
The dragon says go
Let everyone know
You got the touch
You come from Hong Kong   *where justice*
where people are strong   *is done.*
and you won't live long

Chinese Bombs, millions jump, chairman's junk to Hong Kong, USA
Won't Somebody, Won't Somebody
Bruce Lee comes to save the day
Bruce Lee comes the Chinese way

I'm Just a Killer for Your Love

I heard a man who had no lungs
He took me in and made me lunch
He told me how I'd lost a friend
He smiled at me it was the end
I said

I'm just a killer for your love (4)

I cut my hair off in the road
I take my coat off dropped my load
I wipe my hands on the grass
Coz' I know that nothing ever lasts
And I said

I'm just a killer for your love (4)

Look Inside America

Good morning lethargy
Drink pepsi is good for energy
The bath's on, smoke in the bedroom
Sore throat and on my neck a nasty bruise
Where it came from, well I don't know
We played last night, it was a good show

Got the play out on a second rate chatshow
It's a nationwide deal, so we gotta go
Chuck from the company says it'll be alright
Got an add on K-ROQ and there's an instore tonight
Well I build things up
Then I let them go
Got to get time share on the radio

Look inside America, she's alright, she's alright
Sitting out the distance but I'm not trying to make up her mind
Looking for America
With its kookie nights and suicide
Where the TV says it's alright
Coz' everybody's hung up on something or other

"Steppin' off in 20" so the driver says
I should sleep tonight but I think I'll watch videos instead
Annie Hall leaves NY in the end
Press rewind Woody gets her back again
And the whole world could have passed thru' me
But I don't know if it means that much to me

And the whole world could have passed thru' me
But I don't know if it means that much to me

Movin' On

At the music heist
I met the gourmet man
With aluminium lungs
Sucks out all he can

Seek the whole world go flip
In a stunt bug style
He's a parasite
With a cellulite pile
But he can smile

This is the music
And we're movin' on, we're moving on

We're sticky eyes and sticky bones
you get no time on your own
you get a dose and a ghost

You get it coast to coast
dye your hair black
get satan tattooed on your back
pierce yourself with a coke can
put yourself in fake tan now you're in the band

Coz' this is the music
and we're movin' on, we're movin' on
Hey this is the music
and we're movin' on, we're movin' on
no matter how low, there's always further to go
We're movin' on, we're movin' on

We're movin' on, it won't be long
We're movin' on, it won't be long

Essex Dogs

I remember thinkin' murder in the car
Watching dogs somersault through sprinklers on tiny lawns
I remember the graffiti, we are your children coming in with spray cans of paint
I remember the sunset and the plains of cement
And the way the night seems to turn the colour of orangeade

In this town cellular phones are hot with thieves
In this town we all go to terminal pubs
It helps us sweat out those angry bits of life
From this town the English Army grind their teeth to glass
You'll get a kicking tonight
Smell of puke and piss
Smell of puke and piss on your stilettos

Here comes that panic attack
My heart stops, then it starts
Give me a drink
I'll drink your round
I'll take you round the pole
It's cold up here
You'll catch the flu or you'll catch the city
either way you'll catch the flu
or you'll catch the city

Strange News From Another Star

All I want to be is washed out by the sea
No death star over me
Won't give me any peace
All I want is light relief
Put the crazies on the street
Give the guns and feed them meat
Now shoot the death star down
Dig a hole and put it down
Thousand miles underground

They say it's no game
there's strange news from another star
I'm lost, I'm lost
there's strange news from another star

Give me all your stuff
until I can't get up
Watch the whole world freeze
Counting tin cans in our sleep
Submarines are diving deep
I don't believe in me
I don't believe in me
All I've ever done is tame
Will you love me all the same
Will you love me, though
always the same

They say it's no game
there's strange news from another star
I'm lost, I'm lost
there's strange news from another star

Beetlebum

Songs: Albarn
Music: Albarn, Coxon, James, Rowntree

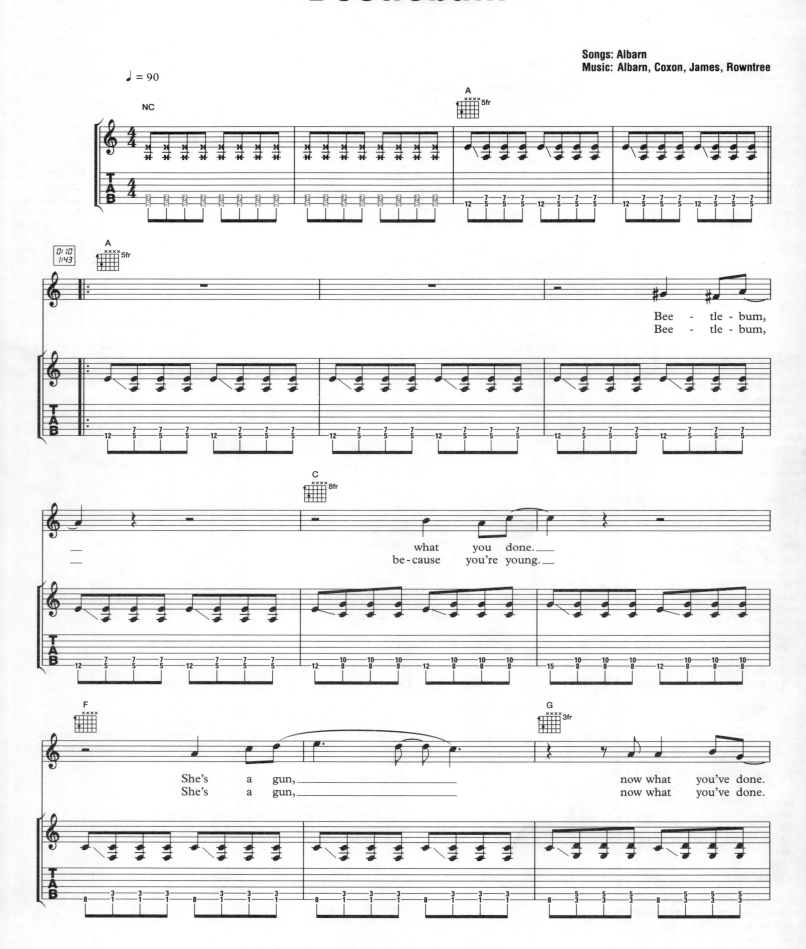

he's on___ it.   He's on,   he's on,   he's on___ it.___

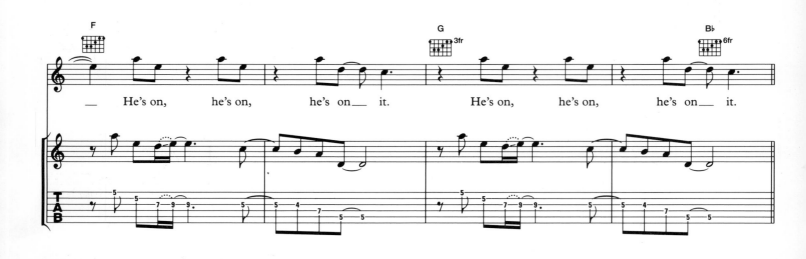

___ He's on,   he's on,   he's on___ it.   He's on,   he's on,   he's on___ it.

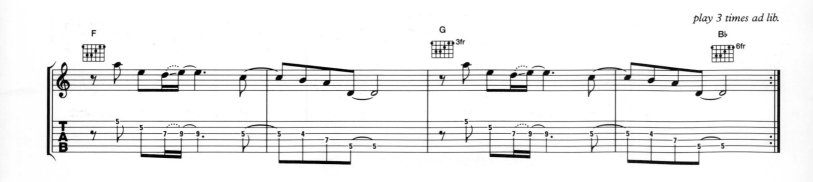

Song 2

Songs: Albarn
Music: Albarn, Coxon, James, Rowntree

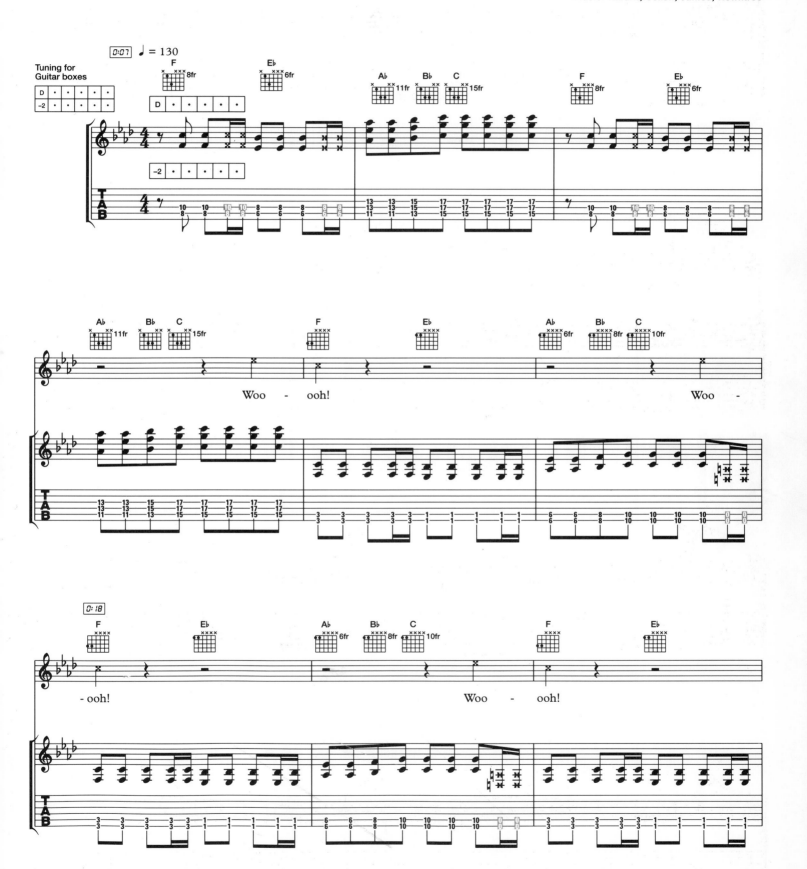

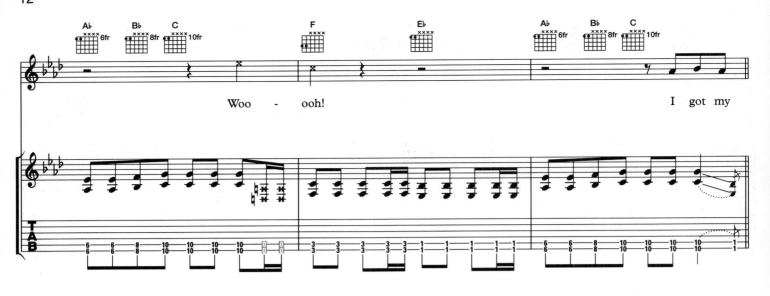

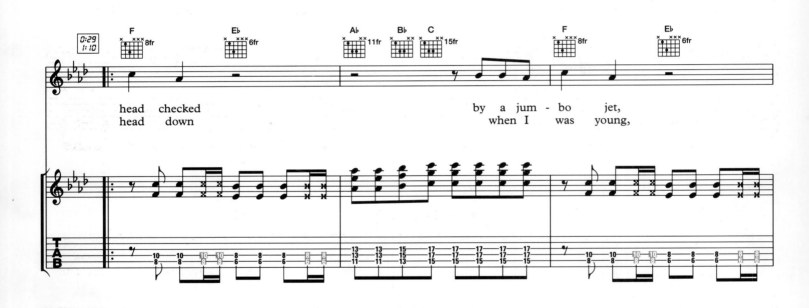

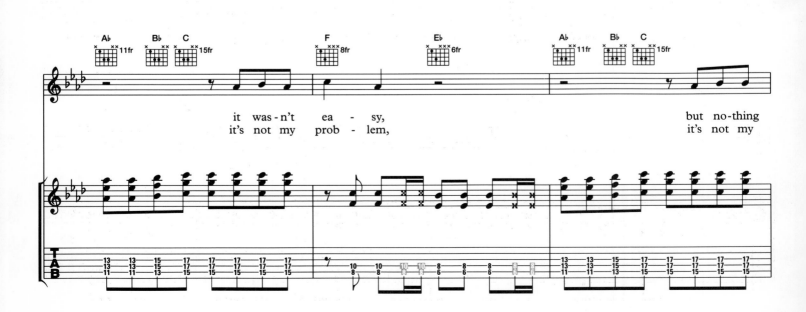

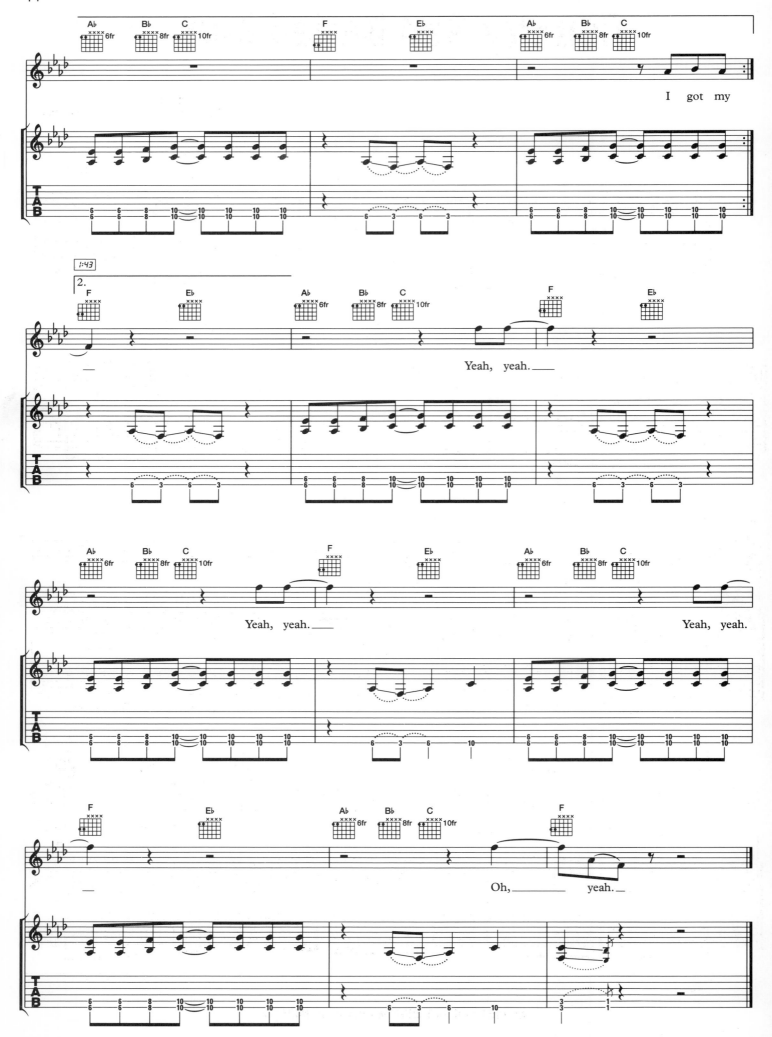

Country Sad Ballad Man

Songs: Albarn
Music: Albarn, Coxon, James, Rowntree

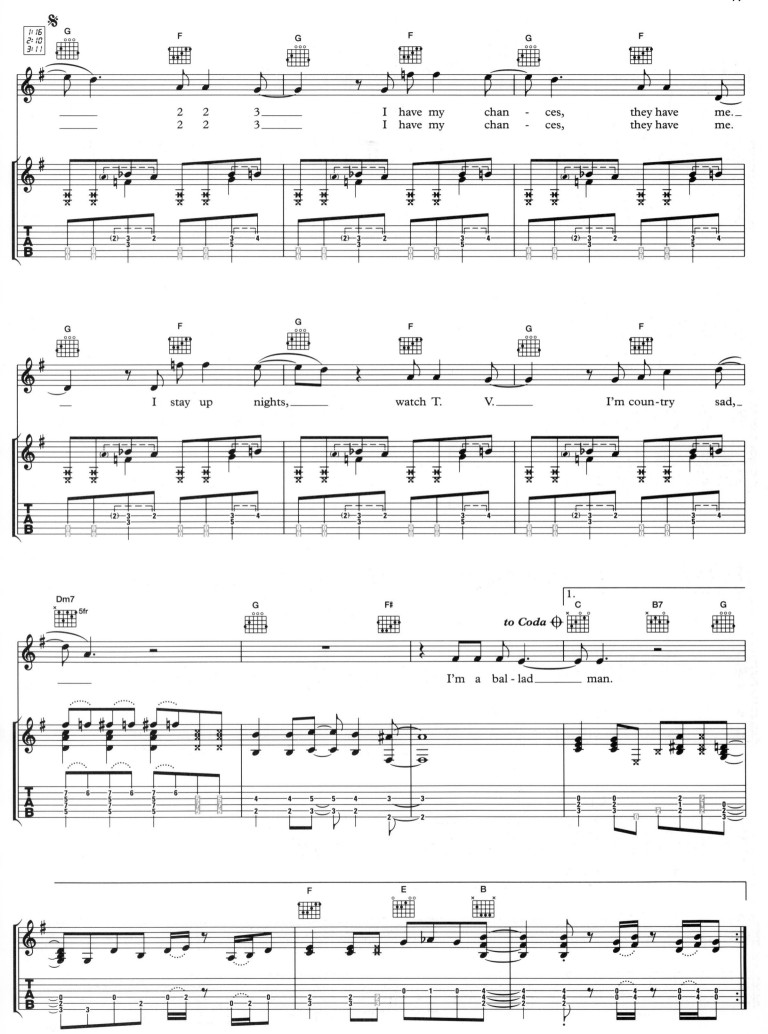

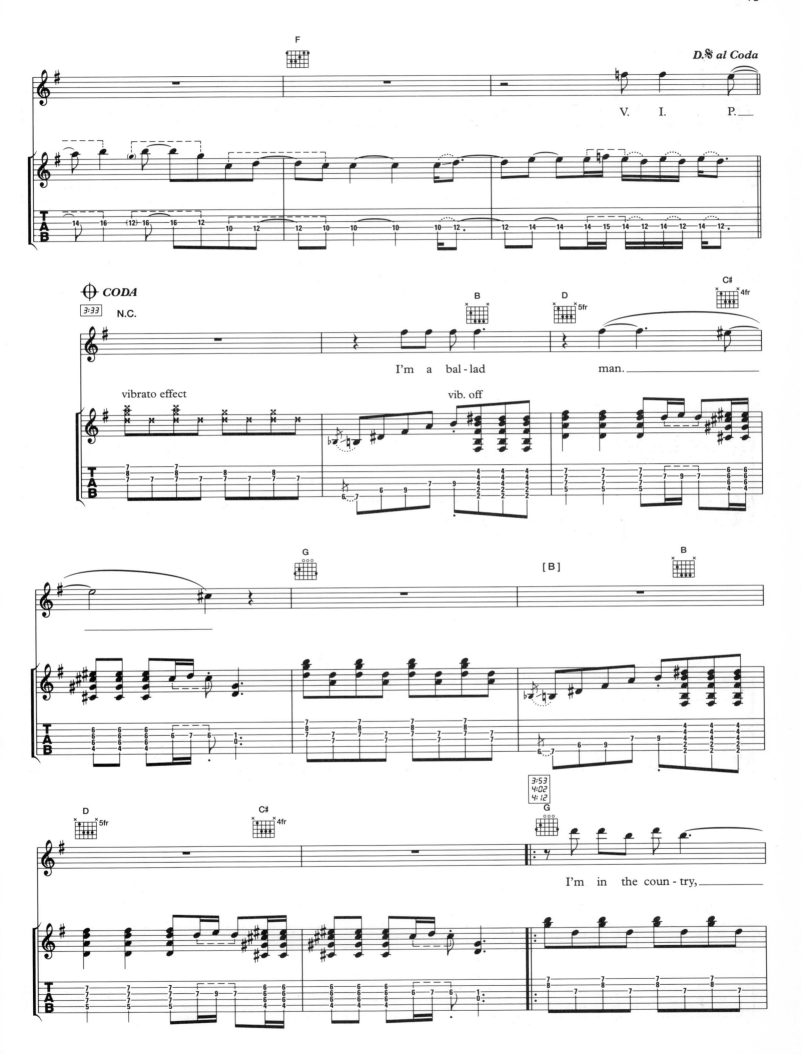

M.O.R.

Songs: Albarn
Music: Albarn, Coxon, James, Rowntree

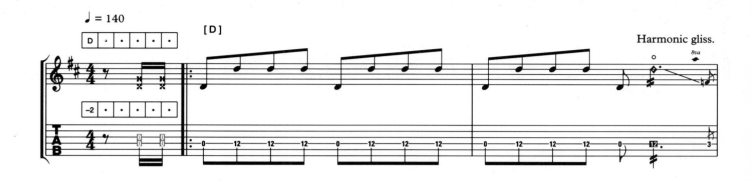

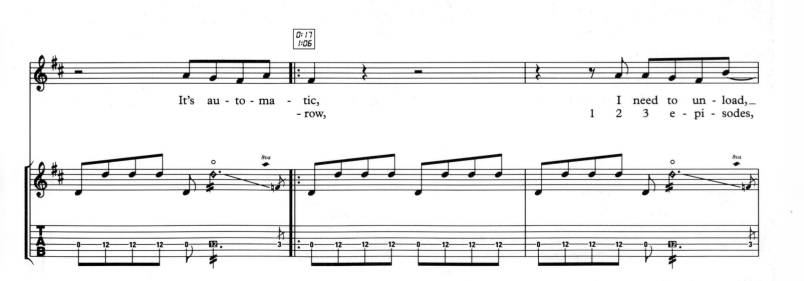

It's au-to-ma-tic,

- row,

I need to un-load,

1   2   3   e-pi-sodes,

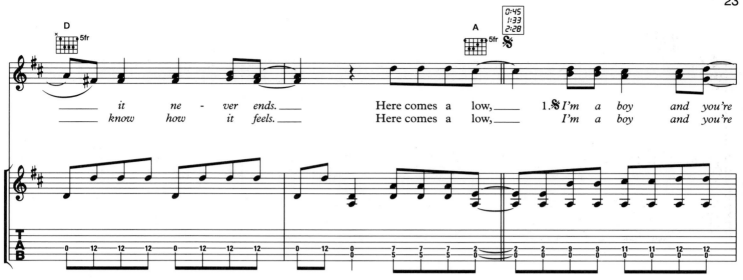

it ne - ver ends. _____ Here comes a low, _____ 1.*I'm a boy and you're
know how it feels. _____ Here comes a low, _____ I'm a boy and you're

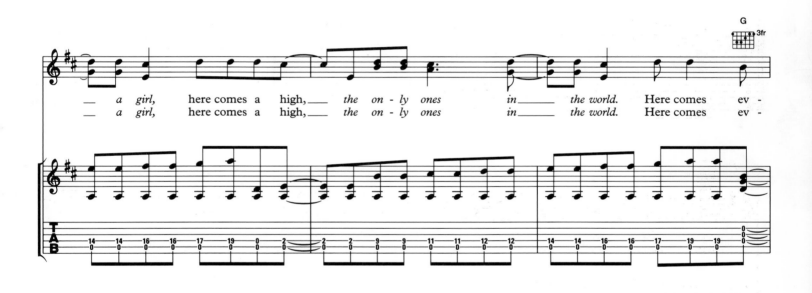

_ a girl, here comes a high, _____ the on - ly ones in _____ the world. Here comes ev -
_ a girl, here comes a high, _____ the on - ly ones in _____ the world. Here comes ev -

- ery-thing, *you and me can work _____ it out.* Here it comes _____ you, _ me, _
- ery-thing, *we're like mon - keys out in space.* Here it comes

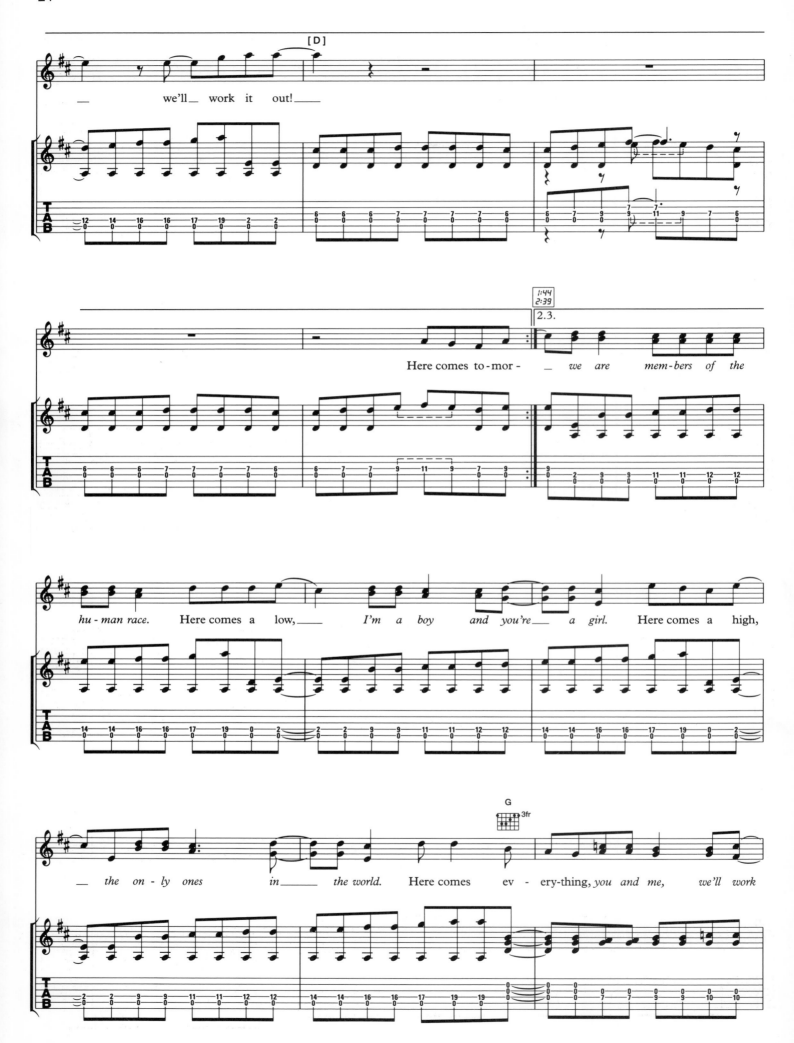

26

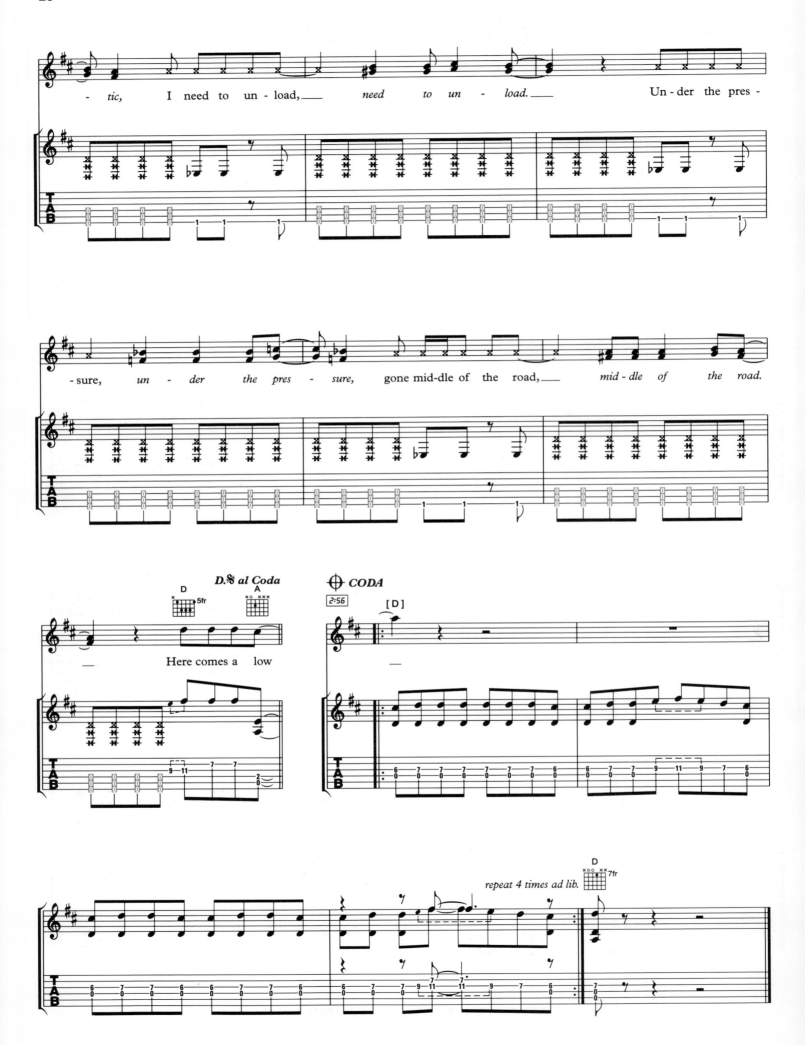

On Your Own

Songs: Albarn
Music: Albarn, Coxon, James, Rowntree

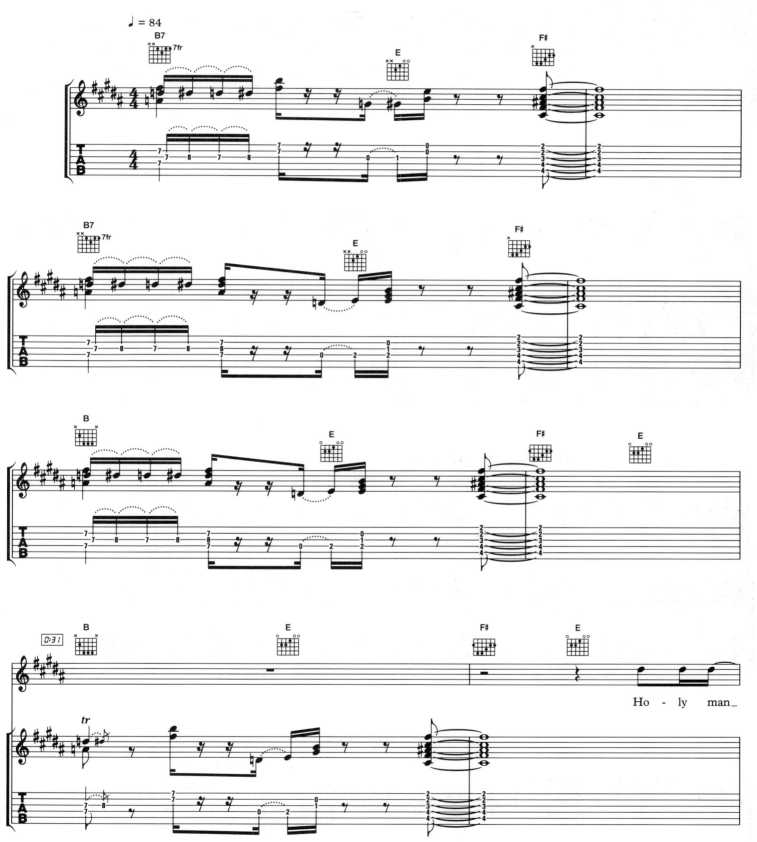

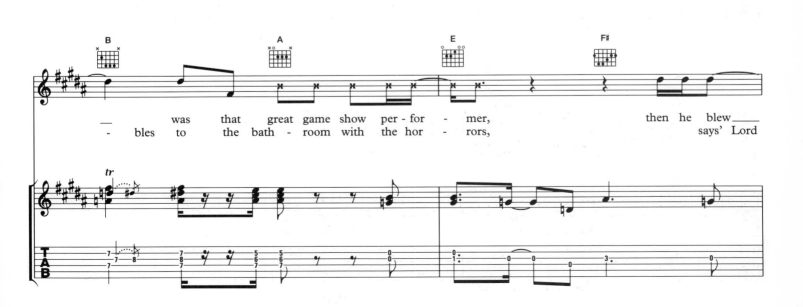

Theme From Retro

Songs: Albarn
Music: Albarn, Coxon, James, Rowntree

You're So Great

Song and Music: Coxon

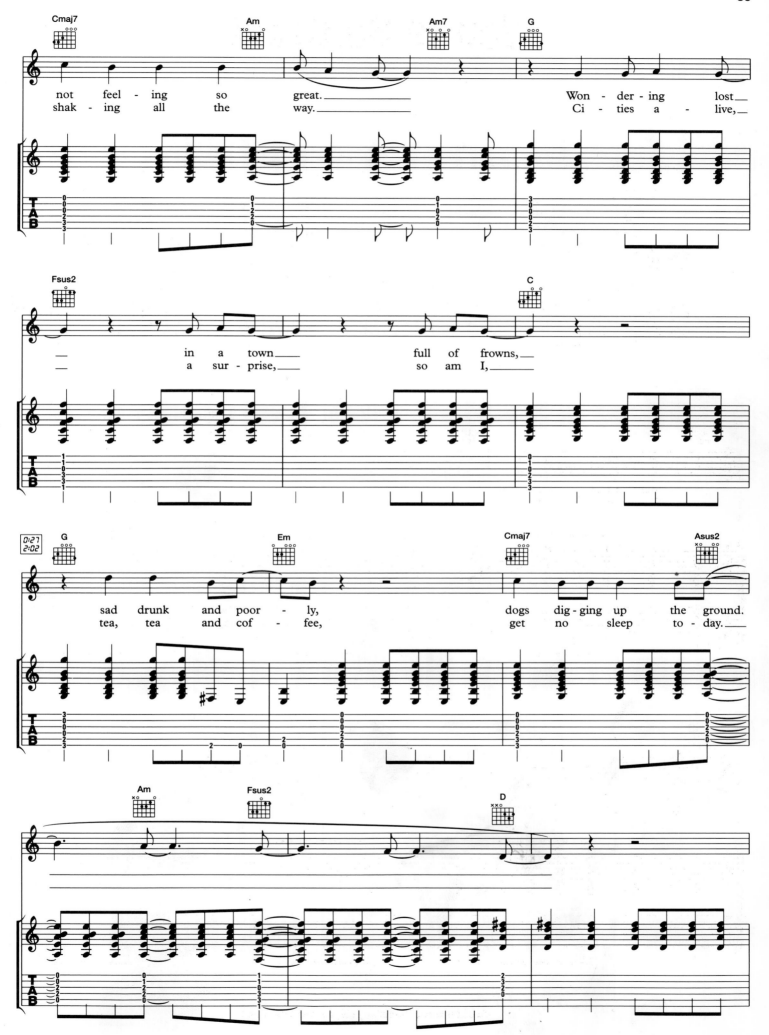

'Cause you're so great and I love you.

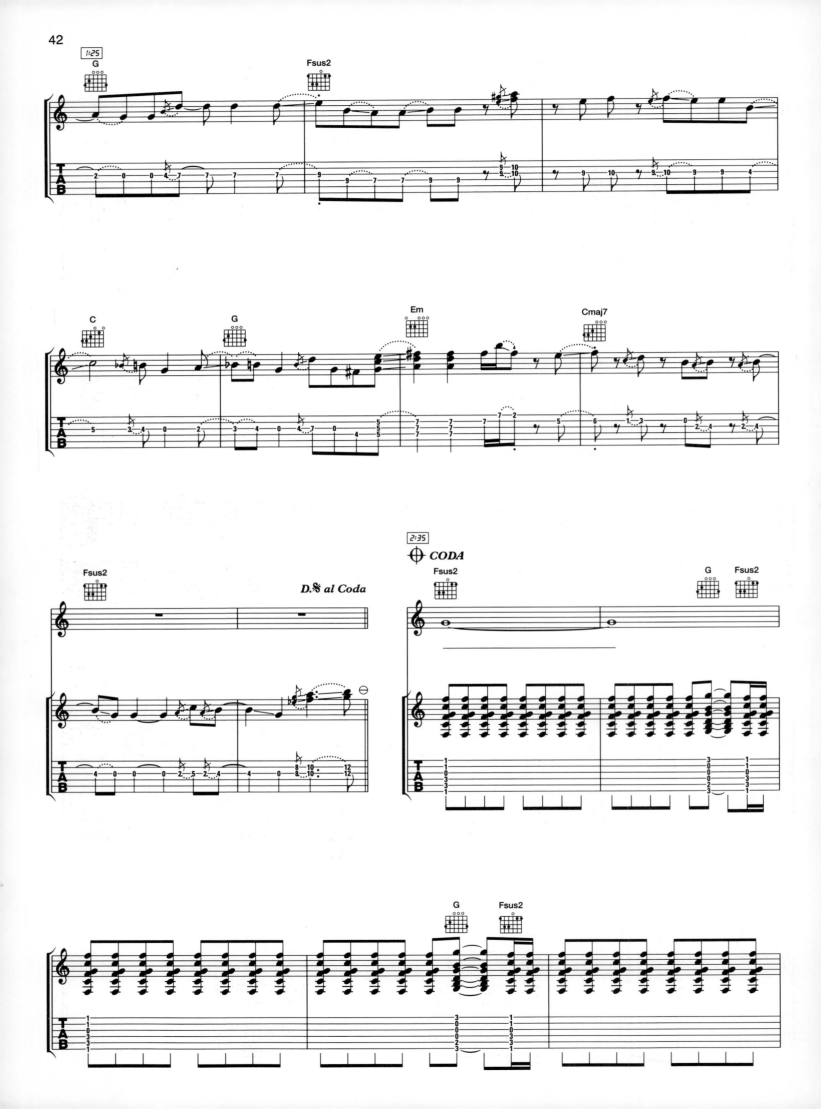

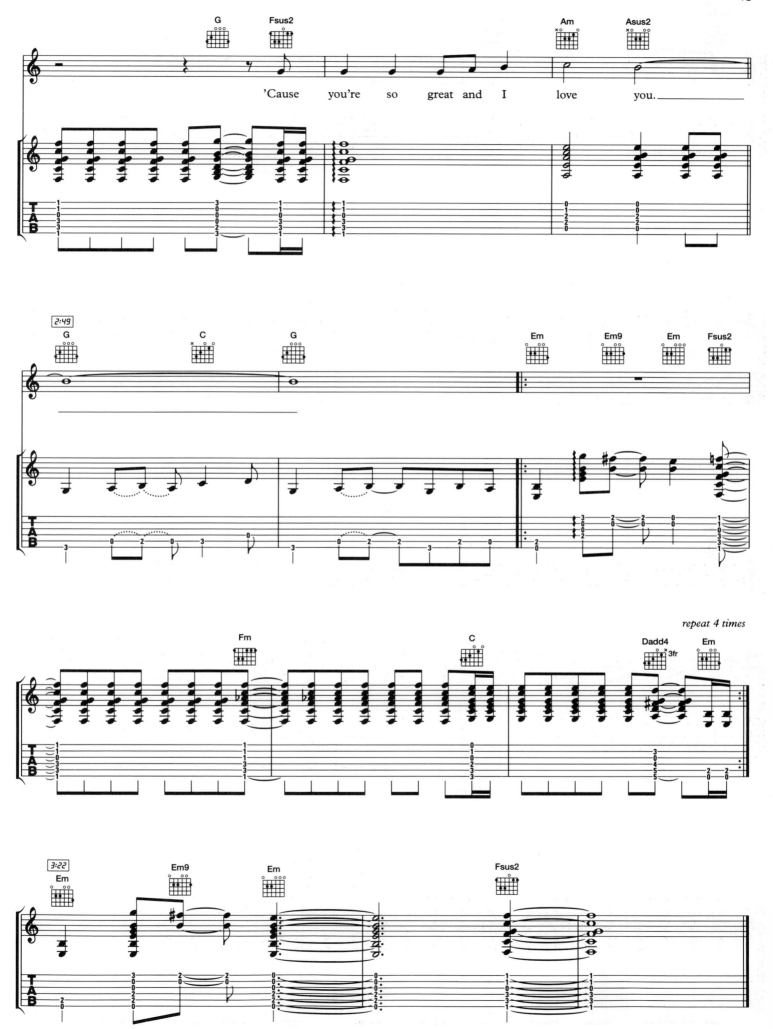

'Cause you're so great and I love you.

Death Of A Party

Songs: Albarn
Music: Albarn, Coxon, James, Rowntree

The death__ of the__ par - ty
__ of the__ teen - ag - er

47

Chinese Bombs

Songs: Albarn
Music: Albarn, Coxon, James, Rowntree

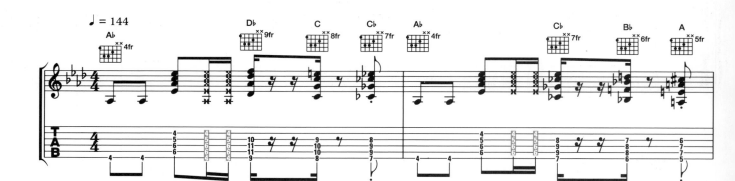

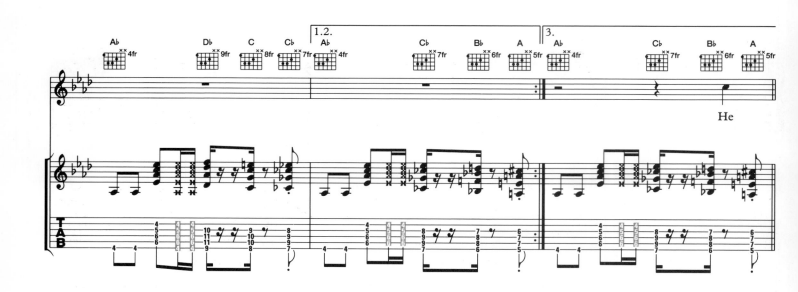

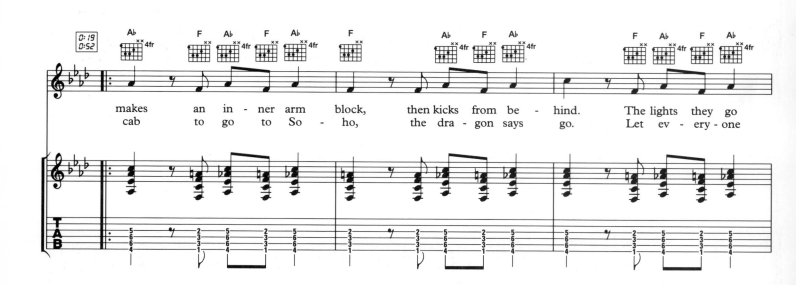

I'm Just A Killer For Your Love

Songs: Albarn
Music: Albarn, Coxon, James, Rowntree

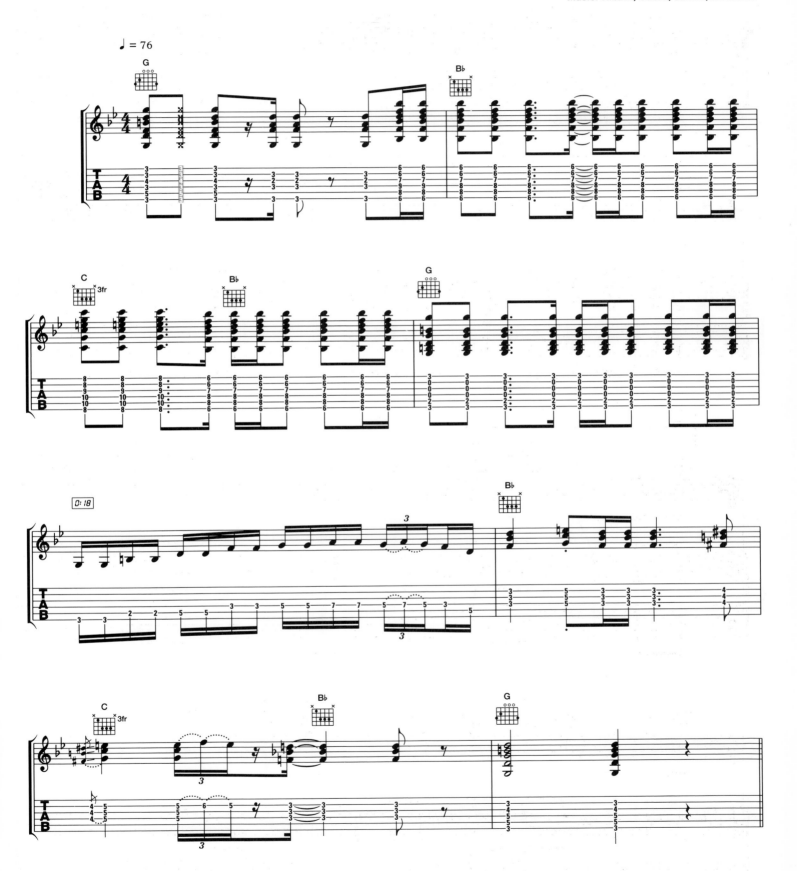

I'm just a kil - ler for__ your love.__

repeat to fade

Look Inside America

Songs: Albarn
Music: Albarn, Coxon, James, Rowntree

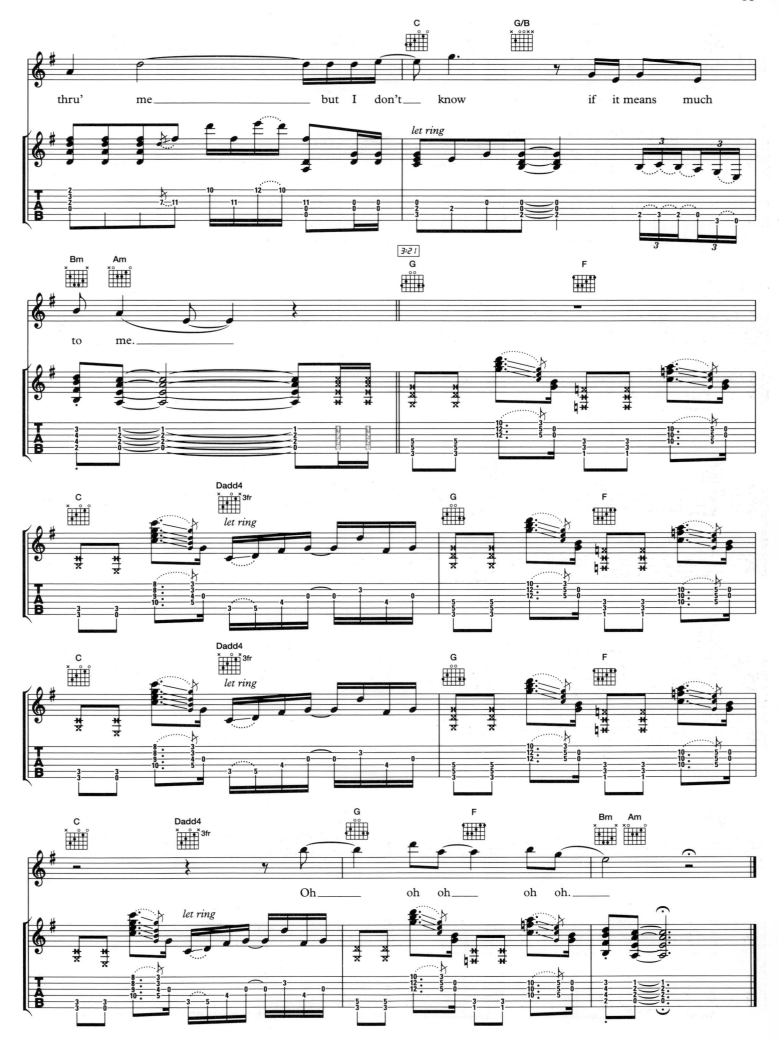

Strange News From Another Star

Songs: Albarn
Music: Albarn, Coxon, James, Rowntree

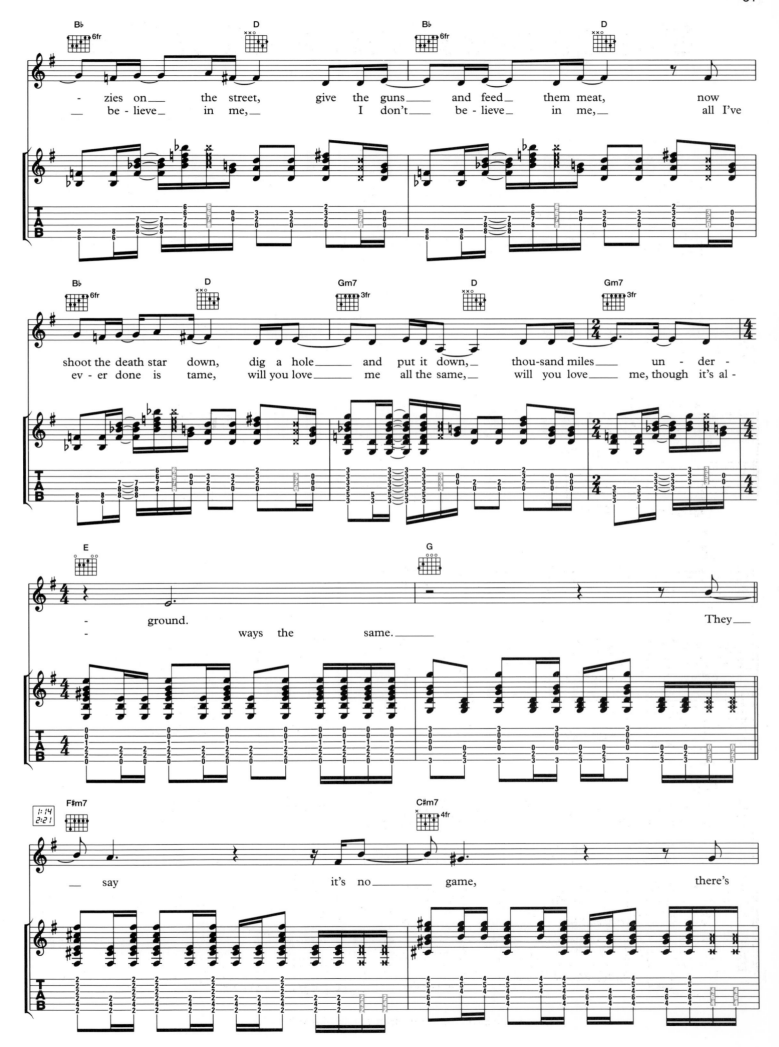

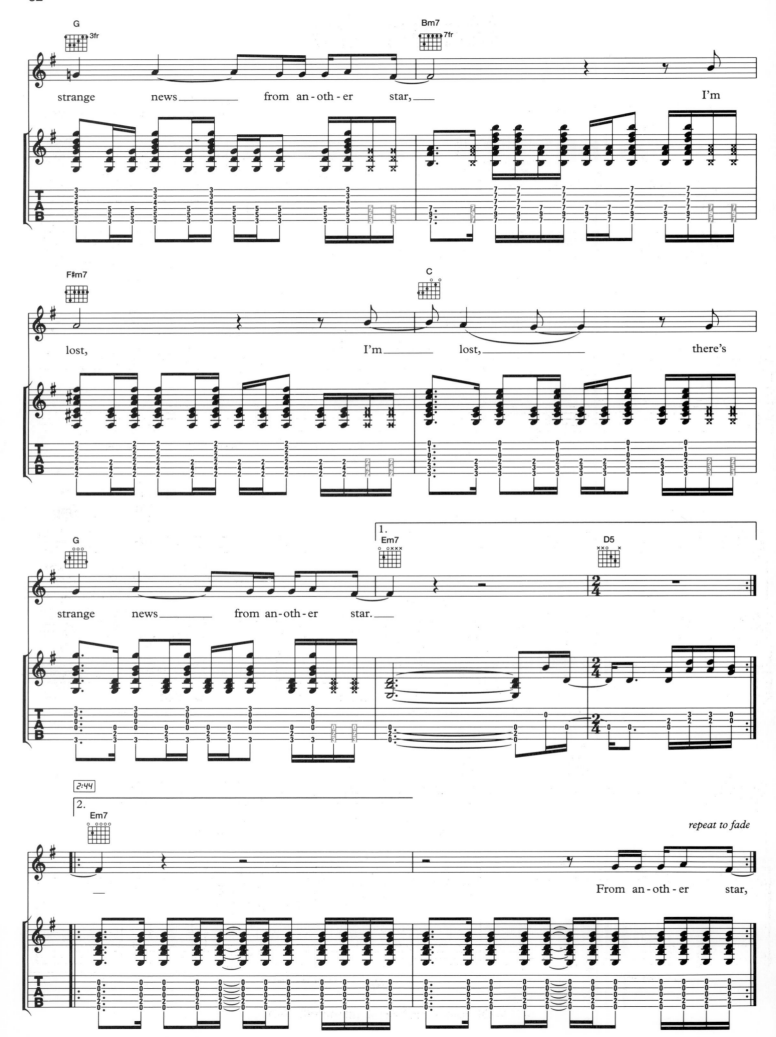

Movin' On

Recording sounds one semitone lower.

Songs: Albarn
Music: Albarn, Coxon, James, Rowntree

66

Essex Dogs

Songs: Albarn
Music: Albarn, Coxon, James, Rowntree

Spoken:

1   I remember thinkin' murder in the car
    Watching dogs somersault through sprinklers on tiny lawns
    I remember the graffitti, we are your children coming in with spray cans of paint
    I remember the sunset and the plains of cement
    And the way the night seems to turn the colour of orangeade

2   In this town cellular phones are hot with thieves
    In this town we all go to terminal pubs
    It helps us sweat out those angry bits of life
    From this town the English Army grind their teeth to glass
    You'll get a kicking tonight, smell of puke and piss
    Smell of puke and piss on your stilettos

3   Here comes that panic attack, my heart stops, then it starts
    Give me a drink, I'll drink your round
    I'll take you round the pole, it's cold up here
    You'll catch the flu or you'll catch the city
    Either way you'll catch the flu, or you'll catch the city

Notation and Tablature Explained

Open C chord

Scale of E major
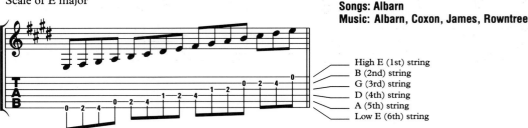

Songs: Albarn
Music: Albarn, Coxon, James, Rowntree

High E (1st) string
B (2nd) string
G (3rd) string
D (4th) string
A (5th) string
Low E (6th) string

Bent Notes

The note fretted is always shown first. Variations in pitch achieved by string bending are enclosed within this symbol ⌐ ¬. If you aren't sure how far to bend the string, playing the notes indicated without bending gives a guide to the pitches to aim for. The following examples cover the most common string bending techniques:

Example 1
Play the D, bend up one tone (two half-steps) to E.

Example 4
Pre-bend: fret the D, bend up one tone to E, then pick.

Example 2
Play the D, bend up one tone to E then release bend to sound D. Only the first note is picked.

Example 5
Play the A and D together, then bend the B-string up one tone to sound B.

Example 3
Fast bend: Play the D, then bend up one tone to E as quickly as possible.

Example 6
Play the D and F♯ together, then bend the G-string up one tone to E, and the B-string up a semitone to G.

Additional guitaristic techniques have been notated as follows:

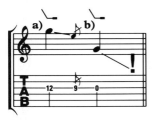

Tremolo Bar
Alter pitch using tremolo bar. Where possible, the pitch to aim for is shown.
a) Play the G; use the bar to drop the pitch to E.
b) Play the open G; use the bar to 'divebomb', i.e. drop the pitch as far as possible.

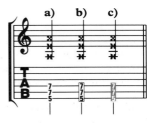

Mutes
a) Right hand mute
Mute strings by resting the right hand on the strings just above the bridge.
b) Left hand mute
Damp the strings by releasing left hand pressure just after the notes sound.
c) Unpitched mute
Damp the strings with the left hand to produce a percussive sound.

Hammer on and Pull off
Play first note, sound next note by 'hammering on', the next by 'pulling off'. Only the first note is picked.

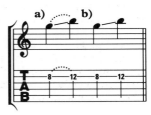

Glissando
a) Play first note, sound next note by sliding up string. Only the first note is picked.
b) As above, but pick second note.

Natural Harmonics
Touch the string over the fret marked, and pick to produce a bell-like tone. The small notes show the resultant pitch, where necessary.

Slide Guitar
a) Play using slide.
b) Play without slide.

Artificial Harmonics
Fret the lowest note, touch string over fret indicated by diamond notehead and pick. Small notes show the resultant pitch.

Vibrato
Apply vibrato, by 'shaking' note or with tremolo bar. As vibrato is so much a matter of personal taste and technique, it is indicated only where essential.

Pinch Harmonics
Fret the note as usual, but 'pinch' or 'squeeze' the string with the picking hand to produce a harmonic overtone. Small notes show the resultant pitch.

Pick Scratch
Scrape the pick down the strings – this works best on the wound strings.

Microtones
A downwards arrow means the written pitch is lowered by less than a semitone; an upwards arrow raises the written pitch.

Repeated Chords
To make rhythm guitar parts easier to read the tablature numbers may be omitted when a chord is repeated. The example shows a C major chord played naturally, r/h muted, l/h muted and as an unpitched mute respectively.

Special Tunings
Non-standard tunings are shown as 'tuning boxes'. Each box represents one guitar string, the leftmost box corresponding to the lowest pitched string. The symbol '•' in a box means the pitch of the corresponding string is not altered. A note within a box means the string must be re-tuned as stated. For tablature readers, numbers appear in the boxes. The numbers represent the number of half-steps the string must be tuned up or down. The tablature relates to an instrument tuned as stated.

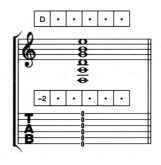

Tune the low E (6th) string down one tone (two half-steps) to D.

Chord naming
The following chord naming convention has been used:

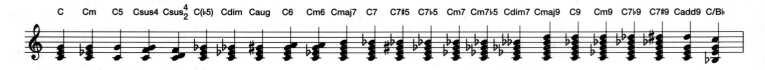

Where there is no appropriate chord box, for example when the music consists of a repeated figure (or riff) the tonal base is indicated in parenthesis: [C]

Where it was not possible to transcribe a passage, the symbol ∼ appears.

Indications sur la notation musicale et les tablatures

Accord de Do majeur ouvert

Gamme de Mi majeur

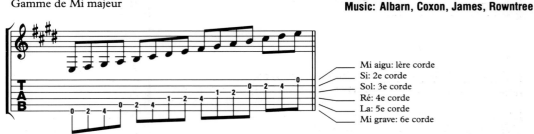

Songs: Albarn
Music: Albarn, Coxon, James, Rowntree

Mi aigu: 1ère corde
Si: 2e corde
Sol: 3e corde
Ré: 4e corde
La: 5e corde
Mi grave: 6e corde

Bending

La note correspondant à la case sur laquelle on pose le doigt est toujours indiquée en premier. Les variations de hauteur sont obtenues en poussant sur la corde et sont indiquées par le symbole: ⌐ ⌐. En cas de doute sur la hauteur à atteindre, le fait de jouer les notes indiquées sans pousser sur la corde permet de trouver ensuite la bonne hauteur. Les examples suivants démontrent les techniques de bending les plus courantes.

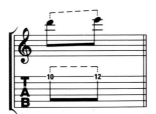

Exemple 1
Jouez la note Ré et poussez la corde d'un ton (deux demi-tons) pour atteindre le Mi.

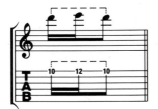

Exemple 2
Jouez le Ré, poussez sur la corde pour atteindre le Mi un ton plus haut, relâchez ensuite pour revenir au Ré. Seule la première note est jouée avec le médiator.

Exemple 3
'Fast Bend': jouez le Ré et poussez le plus rapidement possible pour atteindre le Mi.

Exemple 4
'Pre-bend': posez le doigt sur la case de Ré, poussez d'un ton pour atteindre le Mi avant de jouer la note.

Exemple 5
Jouez La et Ré simultanément; poussez ensuite sur la corde de Si pour atteindre la note Si.

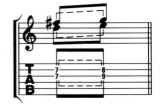

Exemple 6
Jouez Ré et Fa# simultanément; poussez la corde de Sol d'un ton vers le Mi, et la corde de Si d'un demi-ton vers le Sol.

D'autres techniques de guitare sont notées de la façon suivante:

Emploi du levier de vibrato
Modifiez la hauteur du son avec le levier de vibrato. Lorsque c'est possible, la note à atteindre est indiquée.
a) Jouez le Sol et appuyez sur le levier de vibrato pour atteindre le Mi.
b) Jouez un Sol à vide et détendez le plus possible la corde avec le levier de vibrato pour rendre un effect de 'bombe qui tombe' (divebomb).

Hammer On et Pull Off
Jouez la première note; frappez la corde sur la touche (Hammer On) pour obtenir la seconde note, et relâchez la seconde note en tirant sur la corde (Pull Off) pour obtenir la troisième note. Seule la première note est done jouée avec le médiator.

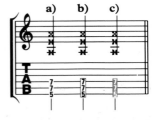

Mutes (étouffements)
a) Mute de la main droite
Etouffez en posant la main droite sur les cordes, au-dessus du chevalet.
b) Mute de la main gauche
Relâchez la pression sur la corde juste après avoir joué la note.
c) Mute sans hauteur définie
Etouffez les cordes avec la main gauche pour obtenir un son de percussion.

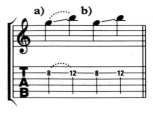

Glissando
a) Jouez la première note avec le médiator, faites sonner la seconde note en ne faisant que glisser le doigt sur la corde.
b) Comme ci-dessus, mais en attaquant également la seconde note avec le médiator.

72

Harmoniques naturelles
Posez le doigt sur la corde au dessus de la barrette indiquée, et jouez avec le médiator pour obtenir un son cristallin. Le cas échéant, une petite note indique la hauteur du son que l'on doit obtenir.

a)   b)

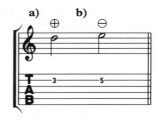

Guitare Slide
a) Note jouée avec le slide.
b) Note jouée sans le slide.

Harmoniques artificielles
Posez le doigt (main gauche) sur la note la plus basse: effleurez la corde avec l'index de la main droite au-dessus de la barrette indiquée par la note en forme de losange, tout en actionnant le médiator. La petite note indique la hauteur du son que l'on doit obtenir.

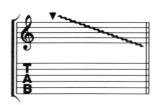

Effet de Vibrato
Jouez le vibrato soit avec le doigt sur la corde (main gauche), soit avec le levier de vibrato. Comme le vibrato est une affaire de technique et de goût personnels, il n'est indiqué que quand cela est vraiment nécessaire.

Harmoniques pincées
Appuyez le doigt sur la corde de la façon habituelle, mais utilisez conjointement le médiator et l'index de la main droite de façon á obtenir une harmonique aiguë. Les petites notes indiquent la hauteur du son que l'on doit obtenir.

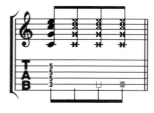

Scratch
Faites glisser le médiator du haut en bas de la corde. Le meilleur effet est obtenu avec des cordes filetées.

Quarts de ton
Une flèche dirigée vers le bas indique que la note est baissée d'un quart-de-ton. Une flèche dirigée vers le haut indique que la note est haussée d'un quart-de-ton.

Accords répétés
Pour faciliter la lecture des parties de guitare rythmique, les chiffres de tablature sont omis quand l'accord est répété. L'example montre successivement un accord de Do majeur joué de façon normale, un 'mute' de la main droite, un 'mute' de la main gauche et un 'mute' sans hauteur définie.

Accordages spéciaux
Les accordages non-standards sont indiqués par six cases, chacune représentant une corde (de gauche à droite), de la plus grave à la plus aiguë. Un tiret indique que la tension de la corde correspondante ne doit pas être altérée. Un nom de note indique la nouvelle note à obtenir. Pour les tablatures, les chiffres indiqués dans les cases représentent le nombre de demi-tons dont ou doit désaccorder la corde, vers le haut ou vers le bas.

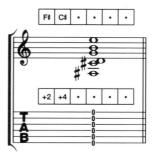

Accordez la corde de Mi grave un ton plus haut de façon à obtenir un Fa#, et la corde de La deux tons plus haut de façon à obtenir un Do#.

Noms des accords

Lorsqu'aucun nom d'accord précis n'est applicable, par exemple quand la musique consiste en une figure répétée (riff), le centre tonal est indiqué entre parenthèses: **[C]**

Lorsqu'un passage n'a pas pu être transcrit, le symbole ∿ apparait.

Hinweise zu Notation und Tabulatur

Offener C - Dur - Akkord

E - Dur - Tonleiter

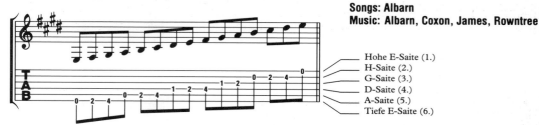

Songs: Albarn
Music: Albarn, Coxon, James, Rowntree

Hohe E-Saite (1.)
H-Saite (2.)
G-Saite (3.)
D-Saite (4.)
A-Saite (5.)
Tiefe E-Saite (6.)

Gezogene Noten

Die gegriffene Note wird immer zuerst angegeben. Das Zeichen ⌐‾¬ zeigt eine Veränderung der Tonhöhe an, die durch das Ziehen der Saiten erreicht wird. Falls Du nicht sicher bist, wie weit die Saite gezogen werden soll, spiele die entsprechenden Töne zunächst ohne Ziehen; so kannst Du Dich an der Tonhöhe orientieren. Die folgenden Beispiele geben die gebräuchlichsten Techniken zum Ziehen wieder:

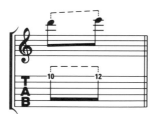

Beispiel 1
Spiele das D und ziehe dann um einen Ton (zwei Halbtonschritte) höher zum E.

Beispiel 2
Spiele das D, ziehe um einen Ton hoch zum E und dann wieder zurück, so daß D erklingt. Dabei wird nur die erste Note angeschlagen.

Beispiel 3
Schnelles Ziehen: Spiele das D und ziehe dann so schnell Du kannst um einen Ton höher zum E.

Beispiel 4
Im Voraus gezogen: Greife das D, ziehe um einen Ton höher zum E und schlage erst dann die Saite an.

Beispiel 5
Spiele A und D gleichzeitig und ziehe dann die H-Saite um einen Ton nach oben, so daß H erklingt.

Beispiel 6
Spiele D und Fis gleichzeitig; ziehe dann die G-Saite um einen Ton nach oben zum E und die H-Saite um einen Halbtonschritt nach oben zum G.

Zusätzliche Spieltechniken für Gitarre wurden folgendermaßen notiert:

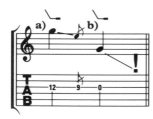

Tremolo
Verändere die Tonhöhe mit dem Tremolo-Hebel. Wenn es möglich ist, wird die angestrebte Tonhöhe angezeigt.
a) Spiele G; nutze den Takt, um zum E abzusteigen.
b) Spiele die leere G-Saite; nutze den Takt, um so weit wie möglich abzusteigen.

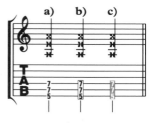

Dämpfen
a) Mit der rechten Hand
Dämpfe die Saiten, indem Du die rechte Hand einfach oberhalb der Brücke auf die Saiten legst.
b) Mit der linken Hand
Dämpfe die Saiten, indem Du den Druck der linken Hand löst, kurz nachdem die Töne erklingen.
c) Ohne bestimmte Tonhöhe
Dämpfe die Saiten mit der linken Hand; so erzielst Du einen 'geschlagenen' Sound.

Hammer on und Pull off
Spiele die erste Note; die zweite erklingt durch 'Hammering on', die dritte durch 'Pulling off'. Dabei wird nur die erste Note angeschlagen.

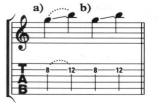

Glissando
a) Spiele die erste Note; die zweite erklingt durch Hochrutschen des Fingers auf der Saite. Nur die erste Note wird angeschlagen.
b) Wie oben, aber die zweite Note wird angeschlagen.

Natürliches Flageolett
Berühre die Saite über dem angegebenen Bund; wenn Du jetzt anschlägst, entsteht ein glockenähnlicher Ton. Wo es nötig ist, zeigen kleine Notenköpfe die entstandene Note an.

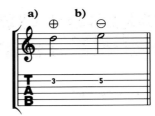

Slide Guitar
a) Spiele mit Rutschen des Fingers.
b) Spiele ohne Rutschen.

Künstliches Flageolett
Greife die unterste Note, berühre die Saite über dem durch Rauten angegebenen Bund und schlage dann den Ton an. Die kleinen Notenköpfe zeigen wieder die entstandene Note an.

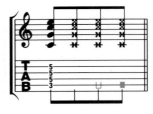

Vibrato
Beim Vibrato läßt Du die Note für die Dauer eines Tons durch Druckvariation oder Tremolo-Hebel 'beben'. Da es jedoch eine Frage des persönlichen Geschmacks ist, wird Vibrato nur dort angegeben, wo es unerläßlich ist.

Gezupftes Flageolett
Greife die Note ganz normal, aber drücke die Saite mit der zupfenden Hand so, daß ein harmonischer Oberton entsteht. Kleine Notenköpfe zeigen den entstandenen Ton an.

Pick Scratch
Fahre mit dem Plektrum nach unten über die Saiten – das klappt am besten bei umsponnenen Saiten.

Vierteltöne
Ein nach unten gerichteter Pfeil bedeutet, daß die notierte Tonhöhe um einen Viertelton erniedrigt wird; ein nach oben gerichteter Pfeil bedeutet, daß die notierte Tonhöhe um einen Viertelton erhöht wird.

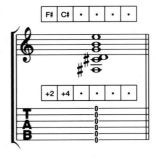

Akkordwiederholung
Um die Stimmen für Rhythmus-Gitarre leichter lesbar zu machen, werden die Tabulaturziffern weggelassen, wenn ein Akkord wiederholt werden soll. Unser Beispiel zeigt einen C - Dur - Akkord normal gespielt, rechts gedämpft, links gedämpft und ohne Tonhöhe.

Besondere Stimmung
Falls eine Stimmung verlangt wird, die vom Standard abweicht, wird sie in Kästchen angegeben. Jedes Kästchen steht für eine Saite, das erste links außen entspricht der tiefsten Saite. Wenn die Tonhöhe einer Saite nicht verändert werden soll, enthält das Kästchen einen Punkt. Steht eine Note im Kästchen, muß die Saite wie angegeben umgestimmt werden. In der Tabulaturschrift stehen stattdessen Ziffern im entsprechenden Kästchen: Sie geben die Zahl der Halbtonschritte an, um die eine Saite höher oder tiefer gestimmt werden soll.

Stimme die tiefe E-Saite (6.) um einen Ganzton (zwei Halbtonschritte) höher auf Fis und die A-Saite (5.) um zwei Ganztöne (vier Halbtonschritte) höher auf Cis.

Akkordbezeichnung
Die folgenden Akkordbezeichnungen wurden verwendet.

Wenn kein eigenes Akkordsymbol angegeben ist, z.B. bei Wiederholung einer musikalischen Figur (bzw. Riff), steht die Harmoniebezeichnung in Klammern: **[C]**

Das Symbol ∼ steht jeweils dort, wo es nicht möglich war, einen Abschnitt zu übertragen.

Spiegazione della notazione
e dell'intavolatura

Accordo di Do aperto
(in prima posizione)

Scala di Mi maggiore

Songs: Albarn
Music: Albarn, Coxon, James, Rowntree

Mi acuto: la corda
Si: 2a corda
Sol: 3a corda
Re: 4a corda
La: 5a corda
Mi basso: 6a corda

Bending

La prima nota scritta è sempre quella tastata normalmente. Le alterazioni di altezza da realizzare con la trazione laterale della corda (bending) interessano le note comprese sotto al segno: ⌐ ¬. Se siete incerti sull'entità dell'innalzamento di tono da raggiungere, suonate le note indicate tastando normalmente la corda. Gli esempi seguenti mostrano le tecniche più comunemente impiegate nella maggior parte dei casi che possono presentarsi.

Esempio 1
Suonate il Re e innalzate di un tono (due mezzi toni) a Mi.

Esempio 4
'Pre-Bend': tastate il Re, tirate alzando di un tono a Mi e poi suonate.

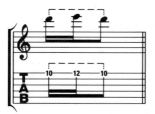

Esempio 2
Suonate il Re, tirate alzando di un tono a Mi e rilasciate tornando a Re. Va suonata solo la prima nota.

Esempio 5
Suonate simultaneamente La e Si quindi tirate la 2a corda per innalzare il suono a Si.

Esempio 3
'Bend Veloce': suonate il Re e quindi alzate di un tono a Mi il più velocemente possibile.

Esempio 6
Suonate simultaneamente Re e Fa# quindi tirate la 3a corda alzando il suono di un tono a Mi, e la 2a corda di mezzo tono, alzando il suono a Sol.

Negli esempi seguenti sono illustrate altre tecniche chitarristiche:

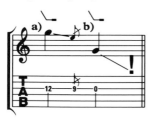

Barra del tremolo
Alterate l'altezza del suono mediante la barra del tremolo. Dove possibile l'altezza da raggiungere è indicata.
a) Suonate il Sol e abbassate il suono fino a Mi mediante la barra.
b) Suonate il Sol a vuoto e scendete quanto più possibile.

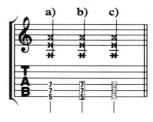

Smorzato
a) Smorzato con la destra
Smorzare le corde con il palmo della mano destra in prossimità del ponticello.
b) Smorzato con la sinistra
Smorzare le corde allentando la pressione delle dita subito dopo aver prodotto i suoni.
c) Pizzicato
Premere leggermente le corde in modo che non producano note ma soltanto un effetto percussivo.

Legature ascendenti e discendenti
Suonate la prima nota e ricavate la seconda percuotendo la corda con il dito contro la barretta; per la terza nota tirate la corda con il medesimo dito. Soltanto la prima nota va suonata.

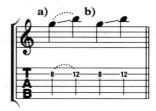

Glissando
a) Suonate la prima nota e ricavare la seconda facendo scivolare il dito lungo la corda. Va pizzicata solo la prima nota.
b) Come sopra, ma pizzicando anche la seconda nota.

Armonici naturali
Toccate leggermente la corda sulla barretta indicata e pizzicate col plettro per produrre un suono di campana. Le notine indicano il suono risultante, dove occorra.

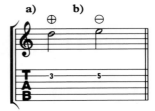

Slide Chitarra
a) Suonare con slide.
b) Suonare senza slide.

Armonici artificiali
Tastate la nota più bassa, toccate leggermente la corda sulla barretta relativa alla nota romboidale e pizzicate con il plettro. Le notine indicano il suono risultante.

Vibrato
Effettuate il vibrato facendo oscillare il dito che preme la corda oppure con la barra del tremolo. Poichè il vibrato è un fatto di gusto personale, viene indicato solo dove è essenziale.

Armonici pizzicati
Tastate normalmente la nota ma pizzicate la corda con la mano destra per ricavare l'armonico sopracuto. Le notine indicano l'altezza del suono risultante.

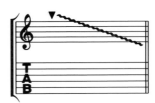

Suono graffiato
Fate scorrere il bordo del plettro lungo la corda. L'effetto è maggiore sulle corde fasciate.

Microintervalli
Una freccia diretta verso il basso significa che il suono scritto va abbassato di un intervallo inferiore al semitono; una freccia diretta verso l'alto innalza il suono scritto.

Accordi ripetuti
Per facilitare la lettura, possono venire omessi i numeri nell'intavolatura di un accordo ripetuto. L'esempio mostra un accordi di Do maggiore suonato normalmente, smorzato con la destra, smorzato con la sinistra e pizzicato (muto).

Accordature Speciali
Le accordature diverse da quella normale sono indicate in speciali 'gabbie di accordatura'. Ogni gabbia rappresenta una corda di chitarra; all'estremità sinistra corrisponde la corda più bassa. Il simbolo '•' in una gabbia sta ad indicare che l'intonazione della corda corrispondente è quella normale. Una nota nella gabbia indica che l'intonazione di quella corda va modificata portandola all'altezza indicata. Per coloro che leggono l'intavolatura, dei numeri posti nelle gabbie stanno ad indicare di quanti semitoni deve salire o scendere l'intonazione della corda. L'intavolatura è da considerarsi relativa ad uno strumento accordato come indicato nelle gabbie.

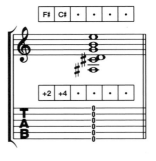

Accordate la corda del Mi basso (6a) un tono sopra (due semitoni) a Fa#. Accordate la corda del La basso (5a) due toni sopra (quatro semitoni) a Do#.

Indicazione degli accordi
E' stata impiegata la seguente nomenclatura convenzionale degli accordi.

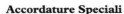

Quando non compare la griglia appropriata di un accordo, ad esempio, quando la musica consiste nella ripetizione di una stessa figura (riff), la base tonale è indicata fra parentesi: [C]

Dove non è stato possibile trascivere il passaggio, compare il segno ∿ .

Printed in England
The Panda Group · Haverhill · Suffolk · 5/97